Canopies of Bones
and Breathable Air

ಐಹಬ

Wanda McNabb

Thorncraft Publishing
Clarksville, Tennessee

Copyright © 2025 Wanda McNabb

All rights reserved.

First Edition, 2025

Published in the United States by Thorncraft Publishing.

No part of this book may be reproduced, by any means, without written permission from the author and/or Thorncraft Publishing. Requests for permission to reproduce material from this work should be sent to thorncraftpublishing[at]gmail.com

Cover Design by Summer Lucio

Book Design by Shana Thornton

Hardback ISBN-13: 978-1-961609-04-4
Ebook: 978-1-961609-05-1

Library of Congress Control Number: 2025935001

Thorncraft Publishing
Clarksville, TN 37043
https://www.thorncraftpublishing.com

For Dorothy and Leland Scott McNabb,
my parents

⊱ CONTENTS ⊰

Appaloosa Before the Fall..page 1
Appaloosa...2
The Barn..3
Purgatory...4
Old Man around Midnight...5
Convertible Hair Sky..6
A Canopy of Bones...7
Spirit..8
Riding the Flatboat..9
Without Tarp..10-11
Water..12
A Valentine for Jesus..13
All Saints Day..14
The Watched...15
Snapping Turtle Summer..16
Moon Rock...17
Des Moines..18
Voodoo Master...19
Carla Gayle is Guilty..20
Scavengers of Time..21
Jinx..22
Cannibals Sojourn..23
Purple Water..24
In the Absence of Dreams...25
Moulin Rouge-Red Mill...26
The Tape...27
The Horse...28
Mercurial Mystics..29
The Goddess of Winter...30
A Good Day..31
Asleep..32
Caught in a Fish Net..33
Adonis...34

Simple Things Like Amoeba..35-36
Little Empress of the Sky..37
Angel...38
Spring Into Breathable Air...39-40
Raging Water..41-42
Ceremony of Silence..43-44
A Night at 1000 Westgate...45
Porky Pig Wears aTutu...46
An Albatross around my Neck 47
Angels Speak...48-49
About the Author..51

ಛಲ

Canopies of Bones
and Breathable Air

Appaloosa Before the Fall

Winter nights before the fall
were quiet as a lone car
speeding across thousands
of stars—a twig snapped by
a raccoon, the only sound.
The wind's howl, the only voice.
Before the fall, Appaloosa
covered herself in blind faith.
The small town sat for weeks
surrounded by lazy angels.
At every gate and door
an angel waited silently
like a gargoyle.
No angels announced the fires that
would engulf the town. Stony-eyed,
the angels watched the townsfolk
fight the blaze. Icy lips offered no salvation.
Angels' wings uplifted no souls.

Appaloosa

The Baptist church tower
leans to one side from the
storm two years ago.
The clock on the Courthouse
stopped at 2:00.
Yesterday's fire has scorched
a city block, the bank, the Dollar
Store, and Mott's grocery.
Hay market town singed
with fire, I see your secrets
piled high outside your doorways,
as dead leaves waiting to decay.
Despicable town that sought
to hide my father's name behind
brick walls, know my hands have
marred your once lovely surface,
turned it to smoldering ash.

The Barn

Brown scarred walls hold voices captive
like a sponge that soaks up water. Bits
of wood are gnawed off by termites and
bore bees. There are strong smells of
straw mixed with animal dung. Sunlight
filters through the spaces between the planks.
A salt block sits in the corner, leaning
to one side, falling into the pile of discarded
corncobs. It is here that my grandfather
blackened my grandmother's eyes,
shod the horse, and whipped me with his belt.
This is the house of memory and blood,
of water and grain, and cold mornings
with visible breath.

Purgatory

In this glass town, I move silently
on the edge of a stranger, propelled
by the wind, eyes straight ahead.
Shadows stick to the trees,
bleed out the light, linger
over the once-green leaves.
I watch a plastic cup dance and tap
down its path; the dance an empty
triumph, the tap an emptier percussion.
A musk-scented dirty man wants to
know if I have the time, the time do
I know it? I say it is winter.

Old Man around Midnight

I hear that old man
laugh as I walk past
the closet door – he
waits inside ready to
spring forward – fourteen
years of not forgetting
his buried-in-his-belly laugh.
I still hear him growl and
whistle for my dog – threaten
to kill the dog – if I don't
accept his touch. I feel
the pain of his hands, like gnarled
pieces of wood, let loose on me
around midnight.

Convertible Hair Sky

On the night grandmother died
Hollywood celebrated the life of
Cecil B. Demille. I watched with
the men in our brown TV room,
tried not to think of her suffering,
no more tea cakes or carefully
sewn doll clothes. Her daughter
clung to her, watched, waited for
her release, prayed for it.
My grandfather had already
lost her, had given her up to Him.
Her son's eyes were dull with her pain.
The house was filled with the cancer
that consumed her, the guilt I felt at
loving her too little, the anger of the
abandoned, left to muddle through.
Only the Convertible Hair Sky was
excited to hear she was leaving us.
It churned and raced, black clouds
forming a chariot to carry her soul
up to heaven.

A Canopy of Bones

I met death in a dream
as I crawled under a canopy
of dried white bones; crawled
like a snake in the desert.
The rib bones clinked in the wind
as I slithered across the sand,
sand in my mouth, stuck in the
corners of my eyes.
I was stopped by death who was
disguised as a scorpion. He left
me writhing on the floor of the desert,
my hand swollen from his bite. He
left me to become one with the air,
the sand, the bones.

Spirit

She witnessed his ghost run
into her kitchen, like he
just came in from the barn
where he saw a snake
or the devil.
He was in her kitchen
stopped dead; he stared hard,
breathed his cold presence
all over her kitchen, all over her.
She stood frozen, in his world,
out of hers. She didn't want to
see the one who pursued his spirit,
didn't want to see the one who
wanted to capture his brown skin
and tattered overalls in a knapsack.

Riding the Flatboat

I dreamt about a flatboat;
no sides, just flat with a single
pole, dead center, surrounded
by murky green water.
I saw no fish jump.
I thought I glimpsed you in the water,
black hair glistening, blue eyes
staring, pleading with me to
save you – I thought I caught sight of your
face, but it was only my reflection,
green and solemn, silently watching.
I longed to touch you, take your
long fingers and memorize the
shape of the fingertips, touch my
eyelashes to your cheek.

Without Tarp

Aunt Euple was big-mouthed when
I first met her. She had plenty to
say about the minister of the Little
Hope Baptist church, plenty about
His views on dancing, drinking,
and ministering. She didn't like the
way he was available for a closed-
door meeting with the younger
women, but needed to preach a
funeral whenever she needed him.
She didn't like his liberal views
on politics, when Lord knows he
was supposed to be a Baptist.
She didn't care for the fact that
he was related to the man who
did the voice-over for Barney
the dinosaur, and she especially
hated the Preacher because
he brought that dinosaur
man to the church and wasted
her good money on a reception.
Aunt Euple was not impressed
by the purple dinosaur man
who ate sausage balls like
there was no tomorrow,
autographed church bulletins,
and wee wee'd behind the well
house next to the graveyard.
Everyone knew he did it and if
they didn't, Euple told them.
The Preacher acted like
bringing a voice-over would
raise his status, make the
good Baptists shell out some

more cash to front the missionary
work in Zaire. Euple and some of
her hard-shell friends said it
wouldn't work, said the Preacher
was a fake, said it ran in the family,
but the do-gooders wouldn't listen,
felt the Lord calling, gave Him their
all and the Preacher their bank account.
The Preacher left Little Hope in the dead
of night, in his blue Mercedes with the
wind at his back. The dinosaur
man was later seen driving a dump
truck without tarp.

Water

The air is thick with water,
so thick that the trees bend
under the weight of it.
I feel the imprint of water
inside my breast bone,
which bows toward the
earth like a withered limb.
The sun does not shine.
Water pools in the front yard
and hovers above the grass,
waits for the earth to hoard
the excess. I stand weeping
in the water unable to stop the tears.

A Valentine for Jesus

I wrote a Valentine for Jesus.
I thought He needed one.
The writing left me empty
like a preacher's sermon.
I sang my Valentine for Jesus,
used an old mountain tune
buried in my psyche since birth,
and raised the consciousness of my
wooden house – my small voice
singing to Jesus like I was somebody.
I made a Valentine for Jesus and
I made the words to rhyme. I said
"I love you Christ man, would you
be my Valentine?" It's lonely on this
flat land even for a powerful god.
It's lonelier for a woman
without a Valentine. Jesus,
would you be mine?

All Saints Day

When I'm dead
Make my body
Into a rattle,
Hollow me like
a gourd.
When I'm dead
light an incense,
chant a prayer, and
rattle my soul.
When I'm dead
don't ask
a preacher to say
kind words or
rush my resurrection.

The Watched

I watched her dance
to the beat of Herman's
Hermits, her Ambush
Cologne thick in the air.
Blonde hair flopped against
her shoulders, breasts moved
to the beat of the music.
I watched from her bed –
watched and remembered
her body sleeping next to mine,
innocent. I felt wrong to watch,
want her hands in mine.
I watched her dance for years
from her bed, watched her
dance, dance, dance.

Snapping Turtle Summer

It was a snapping turtle summer full of rock
hard candy, linguini, road trips, and hair do's
that looked like pink tornadoes. We dreamed
of desert sands and summer places with
descending staircases, of little cottages lit
with the sounds of a rooster's morning.
We spent endless days watching a bore beetle
make his home in the side of our house and
watching a snapping turtle sun himself.
On Sundays we were force-fed Jesus Loves Me
from the pulpit of our church. Say hallelujah Amen.

Moon Rock

I went to the moon,
looked
behind a big rock,
noticed you were
hardened.
I left you
on the moon,
prayed for you,
prayed on the earth.
My words were
carried by a
fierce wind and
fell on the moon.
I wanted you
to soften
return to earth, be
something other than
a moon rock,
full of iron and ice.

Des Moines

I keep a part of my life
cut off, my love for you
unrevealed.
I ache to hold you,
kiss your lips, feel
your skin touch mine.
I keep others away,
afraid they will recognize you,
notice I am a part of two.
We use each other to
remain aloof.
We capture the broken
circle that is our lives on
a three-by-five photo from
our last business trip to
Des Moines — muffled phone
calls, whispers, songs in
the dark are the constant
reminders of love under a
smoked glass, delicious but
expensive.
We tell each other that
we can still play the piano,
can continue to live between
reason and desire, though
our fingers are bound.

Voodoo Master

Voodoo Master
lay hands on me.
White, pink-nailed
sandpaper hands
polish my blemished
flesh like a precious
stone, slowly, missing
nothing. Make my skin
shimmer like the sweet
flesh laid before you.

WANDA McNABB

Carla Gayle is Guilty

Carla Gayle is guilty and a
sinner down to her pink suede
shoes. I see her standing in front
of the meat counter, twirling her
hair, looking from me to the meat
and back again, running her fingers
across the top of the
plastic covered meat, feeling the
smooth firmness, and then she
looks back at me hoping I'll come
over and ask her what she's been
doing since high school. But I
know what she's been doing and
who and all about the abortions
and the boy who left her for a
German woman. I know about the drugs
and the suicide attempt, the
mental institution and the
loneliness. But God she is
beautiful, standing like a used up
waif in front of the meat counter,
wanting me.

Scavengers of Time

Mounds of dead Indians,
relics of pre-history,
newly found dinosaurs,
scavengers of time,
purple-eyed piranha,
teeth sharpened
for feasting; none can
compare with your
muted charms when
you arrive at my door,
cattle prod hands
wanting a stranger.

Jinx

Fat chance of it freezing tonight.
Ponds don't freeze much anymore.
If this one froze, she'd bring out her
skates and turn one, two, three
times around the pond's brown edges.
She'd close her eyes and see the sky
close, as a blue bird's embryo would
see its shell. Her brother would call her
name and say wake up Alice and get
your skates; the ice can't be cut.
Turning one, two, three she'd leap
on the ice unafraid.
Nothing to get excited about either
way as she slowly sops up butter
and molasses between her thoughts.
She craves the ice no less than a
salmon driven to spawn.
I'm counting on a freeze tonight, Jason.
Don't jinx it. Fence needs mending
In the south pasture he said.
No freeze tonight.

Cannibals Sojourn

I saw the world from my little boat —
people passing up and down the beach.
Bright red, green and yellow colors
flashed from the shore like paper dolls
wearing cutout garments. The current pushed
my boat further out into the Atlantic,
driving me beyond the buoy, past the sunlit
beach and into my soul; a gray thrashing place
called home, where Cannibals sojourn.

Purple Water

I see you at twilight
standing in the purple
water throwing yourself
against the waves.
Alone, I watch you
covered in dusk, waiting
for me, but I hide behind
a giant rock, porous and
rough, languid, hard
and cold. What you long for
can't be found inside of me.
Your dream doesn't exist by
the sea or anywhere on earth.

In the Absence of Dreams

I moved into this old white tenant house where no dreams visited my nights. It was a place where the moon in the sky moved 180 degrees in 1 minute, where the books flew off of shelves on their own and where loud music bounced off the wall when no one but the ghosts were home. Every night a thousand restless souls mumbled their mutinies below my bed in the basement, pretending to be the farmhands talking about the day's work. My ceramic leopard guarded me from the would be rapists. My room was a tomb, my heart my only mourner, my leopard my guardian.

Moulin Rouge – Red Mill

I stood outside the Moulin Rouge,
not old enough to enter – fourteen
with a youth's blush – shy thin-skinned,
a girl in Paris.
I stood outside with Madame Austin
waiting for the right age to come along
to enter the Red Mill, to brush up against
a dark-haired boy.
I waited, ate an éclair and walked
with Madame; my world already altered
by a slow dance in Switzerland, three
dark beers and my first kiss.
Later, I would forget the anticipation,
the spring, whispered promises made
at night and life with hope.
I would forget to remember Paris
and the Moulin Rouge. I would
remember only the vision of red.

The Tape

I found a tape tucked in a box,
hidden away from my lover's view.
I was alone. I played the tape
remembering the time you threatened
me if I ever played it for anyone else.
The sounds rose and fell, submerged
and emerged, like the masthead of a ship;
a beautiful wooden woman reaching into
the water. I remember your skin
and the way I felt when your arms
circled around my body. We were married
but not married. I stole the nude photos
of me wearing only a straw hat for fear
you would someday write your memoir and
tell all. I keep the tape as a reminder of you.

The Horse

I stand on the side of the highway, beside the semi tractor trailer rig and look up at the horse which floats through the sky. Suddenly the horse breaks into pieces, neck and head separated from the trunk. The pieces fall and bounce onto the highway. No one notices as traffic continues to move. A horse is dead in Birmingham Alabama, on the side of the road and so am I.

Mercurial Mystics

Mercurial Mystics and
inventors that are mad
and wing-less fairies that
are destined to roam
the earth on bare feet
burst like red grapes
into the mouth of the
imagination. Vivid dreams
that become reality and
hallucinations
play like a fast-forward
movie as easily believable
as dandelion breath
scattered to the wind.

The Goddess of Winter

I drive down 41A and stop my car in the middle of the road. There is an old woman standing on the side of the road and wears a slate, gray cloak and carries a staff. She hobbles across the road in front of me and scurries past the pasture and down the hill. I know who she is. She is the goddess of winter being chased by the goddess of spring.

A Good Day

Today I find a photograph of
a small girl wearing a cowboy hat
riding a stick horse. I find
it in between the Mickey Mouse
swimsuit and the dingy white
sweater, relics from her
childhood. The relics have a
pervasive odor of cedar
combined with the smell
of a decaying old lady.
In the photo, the child tips her
hat, contemplates her shadow.
It is a good day for a loaf of bread,
a can of spinach, or a murder.

Asleep

Asleep, I curl into a ball.
The womb is approachable now.
Fast and deep breath
under the liquid life-force.
Dying, I try to understand the
mask – I must pull it off.
I open my eyes and the room
is out of focus. The breath
slows, becomes light again.
I see the meaning of life and
understand it now. It is the dream
to emerge into this world reborn.

Caught in a Fish Net

A fish net catches me as
I awaken from my dream and
realize I am dying. I breathe
and open my eyes wide so
I will see the last glimmer of light.
I heard you say to die in your
sleep was the way to go.
I am not ready to go yet.
I want to die standing tall
in a shaft of sunlight. Lay
my corpse in a giant bird nest
and let mockingbirds sing out
my resurrection hymn.
I am caught in a fish net
Destined to relive darkness
every night and die over and
over again.

Adonis

Dusk on a three-legged chair
as twenty cats keep council.
Adonis burns garbage in a
fractured barrel, with belly
thrust forward. Harpies sound
their serenade like old crows
waiting for dead meat, circling.
The barrel spews its volcanic
ash as owls herald the night;
two short one long,
two short one long.
Adonis neglects the fire like
he neglects me. He
drives the old Falcon
into the woods to meet
his paramour. Barren and
restless like Medusa I sit.
Eyes turning him to stone.

Simple Things Like Amoeba

She lost it on the road.
It wasn't anything really important
at least not to anyone else.
Purple passion sunsets with shades
pink like the inside of a seashell.
It was a simple thing to lose.
Sometimes simple things are
as important as amoeba to
the whole human race and
animals, birds and fish.
When thinking about why she lost it,
she did not have a definitive answer.
She always had answers hidden in
the top left drawer, under the myriad
of anklet socks; some with pink lace
and some more manly with sharks.
She didn't tell anyone about her loss
and hoped no one would see it on her
face, drooping shoulders and baggy pants.
She could not say his name no matter
how hard she tried to think of it. What did it
matter when you compare it to other
things like what's for dinner or what's
the name of that song that she loved
as a child? It all happened so fast in her
car on a dirt road. The stars filled the
night sky and Jack and Diane was
playing on her radio. Then it was
morning; foggy and moist and warmer
than it should be. He was gone and
a part of her was missing; not him
but the growling underbelly of Cinderella
with no glass slippers. She was not sure

that she wanted a Prince Charming
or even a Prince of any sort. She knew
her strength and quiet resolve like
a sandpiper's day in the sunshine
would carry her down this highway
and into the arms of a gentler soul
that wouldn't care that she lost
something as insignificant as a
night on a dirt road.

Little Empress of the Sky

La Bella Luna, little Empress of the sky
your life was short but your strength
was great. Oh little one of the fairies
you lived every moment like it was
your last. Oh that those who loved you
could aspire to such greatness. Your heart
was supposed to be your weak point but
there was never as large a heart when it
came to the love you spread to everyone
who knew you. We wept bitterly from deep
within our souls when you parted from this
earthly form. You fell silently with the leaves
in the fall . Only six years old and yet
the wisest soul in your beloved family.
We were all family to you and you loved us with
all of your being. We dedicate this land where you
ran and jumped and played, to your spirit, and you
will forever be running and jumping and playing
through all of the seasons. We will light a fire for
you by your grave so that you will never be cold.
Oh that we could hold you again and touch your
silky hair, look into the deep pools that were your
eyes one more time. We know we will see you again
when you reincarnate into a newly born body
 and become your sister soul. We pray
that we will deserve to have you back and that
your energy will be renewed. Perhaps this next
time around you will appear to us as the sun, the Queen
of the Universe, the mother of all nature and the love
of the goddess of Time s
o that your new life on this orb will
be plentiful and long. We miss you, our little Luna,
forever.

Angel

I saw your head on a sign amidst the rubble.
Total destruction.
Were you trapped in there?
Did you forget to warn anyone,
or did you just not care?
I always thought you knew everything
in my future.
It is not complicated to watch over
and save us. How many do you have on
your to do list? I always thought when I laid on my bed
and climbed the stairs to your loft to see you I was the
only one you wanted to protect,
hold close for the dance.
You told me I could get my wings if I just believed it was
true. Was I only your doll,
something you could play with?
You discarded me in the rubble
with my face flattened and
My heart broken. I believed.
Angel.

Spring into Breathable Air

I remember fall as a child and
the frosty mornings out alone
in the remnants of the corn fields.
If I collected enough corncobs,
I could pile them in sackcloth bags
and take them to Mr. Ellis' place
where he would give me a $5 bill
for each sack full. I didn't stop to
consider that I might have gotten
more money by taking the sacks
to Mr. Boggess' place as I was young
and eager to get my money so I
could spend it faster. As I think back,
the main thing I spent the money
on was presents for my mom and dad;
not big presents but things for a
wedding anniversary, like a beautiful
etched dish for candy, filled with
brightly colored hard candies. Their
anniversary fell on the 15th of
October and my dad didn't always
remember the day as anything special.
The sky at dawn was always slightly pink
and gray with swirls in it; an announcement
of the season and of the anniversary. I did
wonder who in their right mind wouldn't
be reminded of such a day if they just
listened to mother nature and saw
her invitation to celebrate. I'm not saying
my dad was not in his right mind...I guess
he just had a lot of other more important
things floating around in his brain, like
would the rain come down too hard and

push the other crops down to the ground
or would the tobacco bring a good price
at the market or would he have enough
money to put food on the table or feed
the animals through the winter. He was
a good man and these things weighed
heavily on his mind and his heart.
Fall every year turned out to be a worrisome
season for my family even though it was
one of the most beautiful. I was sad because
I had to go to school and couldn't play
every day with my friend Patty, couldn't
ride my pony in the sunshine and breathe
in the frozen air deep into my lungs. I
never knew why we children had to
start back to school in the fall when there
was so much going on outside with mother nature.
My big depressions started in the fall and
grew so large and deep by February when I
thought the winter would never be over
that I almost became catatonic by March.
Slowly, with the thaw of April, my heart
also melted and beat with enthusiasm for
the beauty of Spring and breathable air.

Raging Water

Her house had been on dry land
only moments ago and now the
water was raging beneath her feet.
It seemed to be boiling and writhing;
breaking up the splintering wood all
around her feet. Walls were undulating
as she sat in the middle of the room
helpless, holding only a spotlight, her
last connection with her life before
she moved to this river home, discovered
she had Parkinson's; lost her job. Now
this bizarre turn of events. She pondered
how she would get out of this. Soon her
house would completely break apart. She
felt a crash and the water cease to boil.
Her house had landed against a grove of
trees that remarkably stopped it's forward
movement. She felt her face and it was
smooth with streams of tears cascading
down her cheeks. Her arms and legs shook
and she knew she must escape her house
before something else that was bigger
slammed into her. She made her way through
what was left of her door and out through
the tangle of tree limbs and brambles. She
had landed on an island. Her cell phone was
gone but she still had her spotlight. The
rain was relentless and pelted her face. She
climbed and stumbled seeking higher ground.
If only there was some drier ground. She felt
her body going into shock and become cold.
She felt into her jeans pocket and brought out
a snickers bite sized bar. She gingerly ate it and
observed her body start to become aware that she

had many scratches and cuts all over her body. Her clothes had turned pink from the blood. Still she moved forward. Her doctor told her she wouldn't be able to drive one day because of her Parkinson's. She had friends in her Rock Steady Boxing class that had already lost their licenses. It seemed to be a small thing compared to what Was going on now. She was in a fight for her life now. She saw a lean to in front of her. She had a place now where she could get a little respite from the rain. She was suddenly so tired. She went inside what must have been a homeless person's home. She laid down on the dry grass and turned off her spotlight. She soon fell asleep. When she awoke some hours later she found herself warm and cozy in her bed at home. It had only been a dream. She still had Parkinson's and she was still in a fight for her life. She had a chance now to turn it around. She had a chance.

Ceremony of Silence

You and I were made for each other.
Our brains were great companions
although mine was silent most of the
time and yours was more gregarious
and brilliant. I loved to be next to you
and your arms around my shoulders
were strong and masterful. I fell into
them easily and it was as if you fell
into mine as if there was nothing else
to do but submit and feel the tug of
our beating hearts together... and then
we went through the silent times where
you could not talk to me and I could not
talk to you. You did a triptych about it
created from the pain of the silence.
Still, you could not talk to me about it but
just showed me the piece, put it up on the
wall and left me to my own devices to figure
it out. You wanted to talk to me about your
breast cancer, but you said nothing. If I had
been clairvoyant I would have known what to
say. Instead I felt awkward about touching a
breast with a hole in it. We should have had
counseling but instead you turned to your
sister with your complaints about me. You
didn't know I knew but I felt the truth and
it hurt deeply. She was always on your side
as your sister and she could eventually do
nothing wrong when every time I tried to do
something like cook in the same kitchen with
you, I could do no right. When you broke up
with me you told me that you felt like you had
been nothing more to me than a prostitute.

WANDA McNABB

Wasn't I the prostitute who stood between you
and your sister? She came to live with you
and you spent many weekends with her instead of
me — was I not the prostitute first? I moved in with
my mother as she was the only person I had who
loved me unconditionally. She needed me to take
care of her and I needed her to take care of me. The
sad part of it all is that I still love you and a part of
me thinks that one day we could work things out
again, if only your sister and my mother would just
back the hell off — we continue a ceremony of silence
but we talk to each other 15 minutes a week to
make sure the two of us are still living. Somehow
it is still important that we once knew a thing called
love even though we are still silent.

A Night at 1000 Westgate

I trapped a bee in my mouth
It was full of buzz, buzz, buzz
Round, black and gold with
a tiny music box inside.

My gangster brought forth a gun
Pop! Pop! Pop!
Was the bee dead or was I?

The big interoffice envelope
on my bed floated
to the floor slowly
ripping the label to tatters,
each sticky piece landing
inside a beige circle of carpet
silently announcing its delivery.
Dream Reality - No Separation

Porky Pig Wears a Tutu

Three women on my sidewalk
They bear gifts in pastel green bags.
colored hats — red, purple and yellow
Beatific smiles
A wheel of color before me
bejeweled with golden light
The vision disappears
I am left to want more
My eyes close again
Not wise men visiting Jesus
Instead, wise women visiting me–
Porky Pig wearing a lavender tutu.

An Albatross around my Neck

My web-footed friend—
Bird, only because you have to be—
Join me on the beach and listen
To the sea shells or wander
Aimlessly beside me. Shrink yourself
Up and use a strand of seaweed
To become a necklace. You're
Not a pigeon and carry no messages
Endlessly flying because you have
A job to do. Your life is leisure and
Your companionship is all that I
Want. Spread your wings across my
Chest and cry with your loud voice until
The barbarians' souls are soothed.

Angels Speak

Angels speak from kaleidoscope eyes
to announce a patchwork quilt of poetry.
Their voices in harmony join together
and create a dissonant proclamation.
Peace on earth good will to all who hear
them.

 Seeing them is as easy as seeing
a ghost that can't manifest itself.
I once saw just the angel's wings go
by my bed to announce that my dad
would be leaving me within the year.
After he departed this world I dreamed
he was sitting at a gigantic table filled
with a cornucopia of food and drink.

I watched him sit alone at this table located
In a great hall and wanted to join him.
I knew if I joined him I would cross to the
Other side and not be able to return home.
To find solace, I meditated every day to
communicate with one of my angels and
fell in love with one of these messengers.
We said nothing but he held me close
and we danced. There was an understood
language that spoke to me more than
just words could. I knew my dad would
join these angels and be forgiven for his
few human errors.

God would forgive him for drowning the unwanted
puppies while I was at school. I came home
from school and saved the other two.

He would forgive him for hitting the bottle
every day to escape life with his wife and
a loveless marriage. He once told me my
mom told him she wished he was dead
every day. When I confronted her she
denied any knowledge of such behavior.

Angels speak and sometimes if you are
lucky you can see them. If you are even
luckier still you can touch them. Their
words create the elusive world of poetry;
a world where ideas flow and fragments
of thought manifest into a patchwork
quilt. Angels speak if you only listen.

ಹಿಂ

WANDA McNABB

About the Author

Wanda McNabb is a writer, poet, playwright, actress, and musician. She graduated with a master's in English from Austin Peay State University. She retired as Academic Assistant to the Chair in the Languages and Literature Department from APSU.

Canopies of Bones and Breathable Air (Thorncraft 2025) is her first book of poetry.

For information about authors, books, upcoming reading events, new titles, and more, visit thorncraftpublishing.com

www.ingramcontent.com/pod-product-compliance
Lightning Source LLC
Chambersburg PA
CBHW020243010526
44107CB00002B/74